Excellence

with

Simple
Elegance

the study

by Bonnie Liabenow

Excellence with Simple Elegance
the Study
Copyright © 2012 Bonnie Liabenow

Created by Core Communications International
www.coreleaders.net
409 Wedgewood Drive, Cadillac, Michigan 49601

Published by Word and Spirit Publishing
PO Box 701403, Tulsa, Oklahoma 74170
wordandspiritpublishing.com

ISBN: 978-1-936314-64-5

Cover design: Bobby Chamberlain, www.bobbyccreative.com
Interior design and typeset: Typography Creations
Editor: Meghan Dryzga, www.copymoves.com

Printed in the United States of America.

TABLE OF CONTENTS

THE STUDY

Welcome! I'm thrilled to have you join me on this journey toward excellence. Together, and with the right tools, we can achieve a fulfilling life that's rich and rooted in faith, family, and community.

This guide serves as an accompaniment to the book, *Excellence with Simple Elegance*. The study is organized in a series of 24 lessons which can be completed over a 6-week, 8-week or 12-week period (6-week course = 4 lessons per week; 8-week course = 3 lessons per week; 12-week course = 2 lessons per week).

For example:

6-Week Study

Week 1: Lessons 1-4

Week 2: Lessons 5-8

Week 3: Lessons 9-12

Week 4: Lessons 13-16

Week 5: Lessons 17-20

Week 6: Lessons 21-24

Ideally, each section is to be completed by you on your own, and then discussed with a larger group. I encourage you to establish a group of one or more partners to take this journey with you so that you may lean on others for support as you define and reach these goals. I also encourage you to reach out to others and open a dialogue with other women pursuing this path by joining the Excellence group on

Facebook; search for "Excellence with Simple Excellence" on Facebook.com.

Many sections of this guide invite you to fill in words from scripture or from lessons in the book. All of the answers that you will need to complete each section can be found in the *Excellence with Simple Elegance* text, including those that reference other supplemental readings I mention in the book.

Again, welcome to the journey toward excellence. Let's get started.

Lesson 1:

ONE WOMAN,
four PARTS

SCRIPTURE
MEMORIZATION

1 Peter 3:3-4, NKJV

"Do not let your adorn-
ment be merely outward—
arranging the hair,
wearing gold, or putting
on fine apparel, rather
let it be the hidden person
of the heart, with the
incorruptible beauty of a
gentle and quiet spirit,
which is very precious in
the sight of God."

the study

Many times we women feel like our lives have no purpose or focus. The demands of life leave us feeling unfulfilled—discontented even. We feel that we're meeting everyone else's needs...

LIST the people who require your attention and who are your responsibility:

_____

_____

_____

_____

_____

_____

_____

_____

…but our own needs aren't being met.

What needs do you have that need attention?

_____

_____

_____

How do you believe a lifestyle of excellence will assist in meeting your responsibilities and attending to your needs?

_____

_____

_____

RECALL a time of turmoil or disappointment. WRITE a brief description of your story.

_____

_____

_____

WRITE down a promise from the Bible that you held onto during this specific time of turmoil. If you didn't use scripture, be honest with yourself and WRITE your reaction to the situation and how you would do it differently.

_____

_____

_____

_____

_____

REFER to page 15 in *Excellence.*

_____ are an example of excellence in the Christian Life. I call it excellence with simple elegance. Learning about the qualities that lead to excellence can shift your thinking and bring about drastic change, not only in your own _____ but also in the _____. The pursuit of excellence with simple elegance will bring _____ and _____ in your life as a woman of _____, _____, and _____.

REFER to page 17 in *Excellence.*

In your pursuit of a life of excellence with simple elegance, it is necessary to establish yourself in _____ vital parts of your own life: _____, _____, _____, and _____.

In this next section WRITE how you would complete each sentence.

Physically, I desire to be _____.

Emotionally, I want to be _____.

Mentally, I desire to be _____.

Spiritually, my life's focus is _____

_____.

By keeping clear-cut goals at the top of your mind, you will see how quickly the right decisions become clear.

THE RIGHT FRAME OF MIND FOR EXCELLENCE

The Undesirable Woman

Proverbs 11:22 (LOOK UP this verse and WRITE it out.)

_____

_____

_____

READ *Proverbs 31.*

REFER to page 18 in *Excellence.*

If we are going to be women in pursuit of excellence, we have no choice but to possess _____, _____, _____, _____, and _____ in good things.

JOHN OSTEEN'S QUOTE

"If you know God's purpose for your life and focus your energies into fulfilling it, you will run your spiritual race with excellence."

We must choose to run after His goodness.

FIND three verses in the book of Psalms that encourage you to run after God's goodness.

_____

_____

_____

THE AUTHOR'S PREMISE FOR THE WRITING OF
Excellence with Simple Elegance

My desire is to share a simple plan that can be followed by any woman of faith who wants to experience contentment and fulfillment in her home, career, and community. By keeping things simple, you can achieve excellence and elegance. Life is not easy, but if you can simplify the basic chores of life, you can free up time to go after the dreams and desires God has placed in your heart. And once you begin to see those dreams and desires being fulfilled, you will find purpose and contentment. Many things are not easy; there are few things in life you really enjoy doing that don't require practice to be proficient!

promise

Deuteronomy 5:32-33, The Message

"So be very careful to act exactly as God commands you. Don't veer off to the right or the left. Walk straight down the road God commands so that you'll have a good life and live a long time in the land that you're about to possess."

blessing

Genesis 12:2-3, NLT

God's Blessing to Abraham

"I will make you into a great nation. I will bless you and make you famous, and you will be a blessing to others. I will bless those who bless you and curse those who treat you with contempt. All the families on Earth will be blessed through you."

WHEN THE PURSUIT OF *excellence* IS MERELY A PURSUIT

SCRIPTURE MEMORIZATION

Matthew 16:26, NKJV

"For what profit is it to a man if he gains the whole world, and loses his own soul?"

the study

REFER to page 23 in *Excellence.*

We live in an _____ world. _____ people. _____ careers. _____ communities. It is unrealistic to think that our lives will ever be _____. We make mistakes and, if we aren't careful, our mistakes can result in a life of _____.

Our unfulfilled expectations and unrealistic dreams can overwhelm us with grief and sadness. When we have inflated expectations and dreams, we make meager attempts to fulfill our obligations, but typically without passion or zeal.

LIST any unfulfilled expectations you hang onto.

_____

_____

_____

DEFINE an unrealistic dream.

_____

_____

_____

REFER to pages 26-27 in *Excellence*.

There will be seasons of difficulty for everyone. DEFINE what "seasons of life" refers to.

_____

_____

We are in a world of constant change. Life is _____.

Our greatest need is to have something that is _____ and _____.

Many of us rely on emotions, philosophies, religions, and fads to provide fulfillment in our lives. We realize very quickly that everything in this world is temporary with no promise of hope.

God is our hope. FIND three verses in scripture that refer to the promise of hope.

_____

_____

_____

It is sin and the imperfection it brings into our lives that cause us to feel that life is not fair. That life is unfulfilling. Many of us live life on the premise that we are victims having no control of our destiny. And it is in these moments we lose focus and purpose.

READ the story of Adam and Eve; Genesis 1-3.

Imagine how Eve felt. WRITE your thoughts.

_____

_____

_____

_____

There is consequence for our sins. And life is unfair at times. We need to rise above it, acknowledge that pain, and address the wrong behavior.

We need to acknowledge our need for the repair that only God can do. If we begin to seek Him, allow Him to work, and make some conscious changes ourselves, we will begin to see the holes in our lives filled.

RECALL a time you failed and sinned and a wrong behavior was exhibited. Write the story.

_____

_____

_____

The good news is that we don't need to say goodbye to that happy life we once enjoyed. The plan for *Excellence with Simple Elegance* is the answer to finding and regaining fulfillment in your life. It is a plan that requires that we put God first in all things.

REFER to page 29 in *Excellence*.

Simplifying your _____ and having a _____ routine will help you accomplish the _____ of life, which will lead to more time to tackle the _____ that really matter. Achieving personal elegance will allow you to posses the _____, _____ _____ that only a woman can bring to this world. This plan will give you clear _____ and _____ so your life can have _____.

IDENTIFY the day-to-day activities that consume many of the hours of your day. Include the basic chores and the minutes that they require during your day.

_____

_____

_____

IDENTIFY the big things that really matter to you and God.

_____

_____

_____

WRITE the definition of each word. REFER to a dictionary or page 29 and 30 in *Excellence*.

EX-CEL-LENCE [ek-*suh*-luh-ns] *noun*

_____

_____

_____

SIM-PLE [sim-*puhl*] *adjective*

_____

_____

_____

EL-E-GANCE [el-i-*guh*-ns] *noun*

_____

_____

_____

Hopefully you have been able to identify what you do in excellence. What you do simply.

This has also been an opportunity to look at what improvement we desire while we identify the things that occupy our time and take us away from the big things that really matter.

God deserves our best. SEARCH for a scripture that expresses this statement.

_____

_____

_____

Excellence with simple elegance is attainable. I promise.

promise

Psalm 37:3-5, NKJV

"Trust in the LORD, and do good; dwell in the land, and feed on His faithfulness.

Delight yourself also in the LORD, and He shall give you the desires of your heart.

Commit your way to the LORD, trust also in Him, and He shall bring it to pass."

WHEN THE PURSUIT OF *excellence* IS MERELY A PURSUIT

blessing

Psalm 128, Adapted from NAS,
Blessedness of the Fear of the Lord

How blessed is everyone who fears the Lord, who walks in His ways. When you shall eat of the fruit of your hands, you will be happy and it will be well with you. You shall be like a fruitful vine. Within your house, your children like olive plants around your table. Behold, for thus shall you be blessed who fears the Lord. The Lord bless you, and may you see the prosperity all the days of your life. Indeed, may you see your children's children. Peace be upon God's people!

Lesson 3:

THE FOUNDATION OF
excellence

SCRIPTURE
MEMORIZATION

John 3:16, NKJV

*"For God so loved the
world that He gave His
only begotten Son, that
whoever believes in Him
should not perish but
have everlasting life."*

the study

THE FIRST STEP TO ATTAINING A
LIFE OF EXCELLENCE IS ESTABLISH-
ING A FOUNDATION FOR THE LIFE
YOU DESIRE TO LIVE.

A solid foundation keeps you
focused and outlines your priori-
ties. The foundation of living a life
centered in biblical principals is
constructed in this order: faith,
family, and community.

HERE IS WHERE YOU WILL DEVELOP
THE SPIRITUAL ASPECT OF YOUR LIFE.

WRITE your statement of faith.

_____

_____

_____

IDENTIFY your life verse from scripture.

_____

_____

_____

_____

READ the book of Ruth.

Ruth was committed to establishing a new foundation for her life—different from the life she lived in Moab. Ruth made a heartfelt statement, one of faith and commitment. This foundational statement set her on a course toward fulfillment and into God's purpose for her life.

IDENTIFY Ruth's foundational statement.

_____

_____

_____

_____

_____

REFER to page 33 in *Excellence*.

There are three parts to the foundation of excellence:

_____, _____, and

_____.

promise

2 Corinthians 5:17, CEV

"Anyone who belongs to Christ is a new person. The past is forgotten, and everything is new."

blessing

Numbers 6:24-26, NLT

"May the Lord bless you and protect you. May the Lord smile on you and be gracious to you. May the Lord show you his favor and give you his peace."

Lesson 4:
FAITH

SCRIPTURE
MEMORIZATION

Ruth 1:16, CEV

"...Your God will be my God...." (Ruth's words of commitment to her faith.)

Romans 10:9 and 10:13, NKJV

"...That if you confess with your mouth the Lord Jesus and believe in your heart that God has raised Him from the dead, you will be saved."

"For 'whoever calls on the name of the LORD shall be saved.'"

Hebrews 11:1, NKJV

"Now faith is the substance of things hoped for, the evidence of things not seen."

the study

This simple, foundational statement leads Ruth to a life of purpose and fulfillment.

REFER to page 37 in *Excellence*.

Note the three points of sacrifice Ruth gave to this commitment:

1. _____
   _____

2. _____
   _____

3. _____
   _____

This sacrifice demonstrates her _____ and _____ to her number-one priority, GOD.

WRITE the story of when you first committed your life to God and received Jesus into your heart.

_____

_____

_____

The first-time commitment to God is always significant and memorable. However, it is our constant demonstration of this commitment, consciously and on a daily basis, that shows our obedience. We must commit and recommit to our foundation.

Renew your mind daily.

WRITE down a scripture that instructs us to renew our minds to biblical truth.

_____

_____

_____

_____

2 Corinthians 5:17

WRITE this scripture out and then SHARE what it means to you.

_____

_____

_____

_____

promise

Ephesians 2:8, NLV

"For by His loving-favor you have been saved from the punishment of sin through faith. It is not by anything you have done. It is a gift of God."

blessing

Sabbath Prayer (From the musical play *Fiddler on the Roof*)

May the Lord protect and defend you,
May He always shield you from shame;
May you come to be in Israel a shining name.
May you be like Ruth and like Esther,
May you be deserving of praise;
Strengthen them, oh Lord, and keep them from the stranger's ways.

May God bless you and grant you long lives,
May the Lord fulfill our Sabbath prayer for you.
May God make you good mothers and wives.
May He send you husbands who will care for you.
May the Lord protect and defend you,
May the Lord preserve you from pain;
Favor them, oh Lord, with happiness and peace,
Oh hear our Sabbath prayer. Amen.

Lesson 5:

PUT GOD *first*

SCRIPTURE
MEMORIZATION

Proverbs 3:6, TLB

"In everything you do, put God first, and He will direct you and crown your efforts with success."

the study

ASK yourself these three questions.
REFER to page 39 in *Excellence*.

1. Am I willing to _____
   _____
   _____
   to accomplish God's best will for my life?

2. Am I willing to _____
   _____
   _____
   that come with a life that is passionate for God?

3. Am I willing to _____
   _____
   _____
   to His call and His plan for my life?

If you can honestly say "YES" to all three questions, you have just laid the foundation for a life of excellence.

Now the provision God's _____, _____, and _____ is available to you.

Moved by her newfound faith in the God of Israel, this young Moabite woman, Ruth, left familiarity to embrace the unfamiliar. May we have willing hearts like Ruth to move to the unfamiliar when God calls us there. Faith and blessing is seldom familiar or comfortable, but God's presence is its worthy reward.

When you are willing to step out in faith into unfamiliar circumstances, God's presence in your life will give you guidance.

RETURN to the story of Ruth. WRITE in your own words how God moved her into the unfamiliar.

_____

_____

_____

RECALL a time when you had to step into the unfamiliar and it was outside of your comfort zone. DESCRIBE how you felt.

_____

_____

_____

When you feel God is calling you to do something, follow Him outside of your protective world and hear His message to you. As if He's saying "I have something bigger for you;" He knows you have a desire for something in your heart. This is an important opportunity for many reasons.

LIST the reasons you believe God intentionally moved you from familiar to unfamiliar.

_____

_____

_____

REFER to pages 40-42 in *Excellence*.

When we are outside of our comfort zone, we cannot forget that we have immediate access to God through _____, _____, and _____.

Isaiah 28:29, NKJV

"This also comes from the Lord of Hosts, Who is wonderful in counsel and excellent in guidance."

IT IS YOUR CHOICE TO WALK IN HIS GUIDANCE AND COUNSEL. God is a gentleman, He never forces His will or way into one's heart.

God will give counsel when _____
to give Him your _____ and _____
to listen.

Every time you make any decision, _____, or
_____, seek His will. But be prepared that the
right choice for your life may not be the _____
choice to make, but the _____ will always be in
line with _____.

Sacrifice and extending yourself beyond your comfort zone
is all part of the experience that comes along with your
newly established foundation and your commitment to
follow His path.

The act of obedience can be simple.

GIVE examples of sacrifices you made to be obedient to His
call to the unfamiliar in your life.

_____

_____

_____

_____

Faith and blessing is seldom familiar or comfortable. But
God's presence is its worthy reward.

SHARE how God's presence in the unfamiliar was your reward and how He guided you.

_____

_____

_____

_____

_____

_____

_____

_____

It is with these acts of obedience, you will find such freedom, joy and tremendous peace of mind to your soul and spirit— just knowing that you are in God's will. You do have the choice to make your life one that has purpose. His purpose.

It is within the moments and seasons of unfamiliar that we allow ourselves to be totally dependent on God. When we lend to His guidance and operate in His will for our life, we become in tune to our gifting—our talents, our anointed spiritual gifting.

With commitment comes great responsibility. In those responsibilities, God provides strength.

Psalm 28:8, The Message
"God is all strength for his people."

RETURN to the story of Ruth. WRITE about the responsibilities given to her.

_____

_____

_____

God's presence in our lives gives us the strength and confidence to handle all of life's responsibilities.

WRITE down your life's responsibilities.

_____

_____

_____

WRITE the promise of *Psalm 29:11*.

_____

_____

_____

WRITE a story in your life or in the life of someone you know where God provided strength.

_____

_____

_____

_____

_____

_____

FIND three more verses in which God promises strength to His people.

_____

_____

_____

_____

_____

_____

When obedience becomes a part of your total commitment, you will have access to God's loving protection in all your pursuits.

1 Samuel 25:29, The Message

"Know this: Your God-honored life is tightly bound in the bundle of God-protected life."

WRITE what this verse means to you concerning God's protective covering in your life.

_____

_____

REVIEW the story of Ruth. WRITE down how God provided for and protected Ruth.

_____

_____

God's protective canopy is for those who remain obedient and faithful to Him, and He will apply that protection to every area of your life.

Psalm 121:5, The Message
"God's your Guardian, right at your side to protect you."

WRITE how you believe God protects us in each of these areas. FIND two verses that reflect the promises of God's protection in each of these areas.

PHYSICAL PROTECTION

_____

_____

_____

EMOTIONAL PROTECTION

_____

_____

_____

MENTAL PROTECTION

_____

_____

_____

SPIRITUAL PROTECTION

_____

_____

_____

Your act of faith and being in His Word daily leads to understanding His will for your life. Understanding His will gives purpose for this earthly life. This established foundation delivers the guidance, strength, and protection needed for a life of excellence. Your life is no longer about your needs and you—it's about sharing God's love.

WRITE your story about how you reached out to someone or someone reached out to you that was an act of obedience to God.

_____

_____

_____

_____

_____

_____

_____

_____

_____

_____

_____

promise

Isaiah 1:19, CEV

"If you willingly obey me, the best crops in the land will be yours."

blessing

2 Thessalonians 2:16-17, NKJV

"Now may our Lord Jesus Christ Himself, and our God and Father, who has loved us and given us everlasting consolation and good hope by grace, comfort your hearts and establish you in every good word and work."

Lesson 6:

FAMILY

SCRIPTURE
MEMORIZATION

Ruth 1:16, CEV

*"...Your people will be
my people...." (Ruth's
statement of her
commitment to family.)*

the study

A sincere commitment to make
your family the first priority above
all human relationships is the
second step in building the foundation that leads to a life of excellence with simple elegance.

Deuteronomy 5:16,
NKJV

*"Honor your father and
your mother, as the
LORD your God has
commanded you, that
your days may be long,
and that it may be well
with you in the land
which the LORD your
God is giving you."*

Let's REFLECT again on the story
of Ruth.

DESCRIBE how Ruth demonstrated
a commitment to family.

_____

_____

_____

_____

_____

_____

_____

Ruth 3:5, NKJV

"All that you say to me I will do."

WRITE what you think Ruth meant by this statement.

_____

_____

_____

Unfortunately society has not considered the necessity of nurturing intimacy, communication, and commitment within the family.

REFER to Barna Research Group online for new statistics or page 52 in *Excellence*.

GIVE statistics/facts that support this statement.

_____

_____

REFER to page 53 in *Excellence*.

The greatest human need is _____.

JESUS BLESSES THE CHILDREN

Mark 10:13-16, NKJV

"Then they brought little children to Him, that He might touch them; but the disciples rebuked those who brought them. But when Jesus saw it, He

was greatly displeased and said to them, 'Let the little children come to Me, and do not forbid them; for of such is the kingdom of God. Assuredly, I say to you, whoever does not receive the kingdom of God as a little child will by no means enter it.' And He took them up in His arms, laid His hands on them, and blessed them."

Blessing our children is as vital in today's world as it was in Jesus' time. With temptations and pressure in our society pulling at them, children need a wall of protection and love surrounding them. This wall can be built by the practice of "the blessing."

REFER to page 54 in *Excellence*.

THE BLESSING

IDENTIFY the five keys to passing on the blessing to your family.

1. _____

2. _____

3. _____

4. _____

5. _____

These five elements became the tool that I used to enhance the way I communicated love and acceptance to my sons. Bestowing the blessing was a model of behavior I wanted to exhibit. So I made a conscious decision to make a daily practice of blessing my children.

YOUR ASSIGNMENT: Bestow the blessing on your children or spouse this week using the five key elements, and journal the experience. Come prepared to share. WRITE down the elements of the blessing that were used to bless your family.

Your children and spouse do have a special future. God has a wonderful plan for them. Bestowing the blessing on each child and your spouse will show your commitment to them and their future. Exercising the elements of the blessing can also be the source of communicating approval, not just to your family but to others as well.

Jeremiah 29:11, The Living Bible

"Know the plans He has for you. For good and not for evil, to give you a future and a hope."

WRITE how the message of this verse is a promise for your children.

_____

_____

_____

If you are constantly striving to release the blessing into the lives of those around you, you will be operating with loyalty and commitment to your family.

It is this servant heart that will lead you to the excellence God has for you.

promise
Proverbs 22:6, NKJV

"Train up a child in the way he should go, and when he is old he will not depart from it."

blessing
Isaiah 44:3 (NLV)

"For I will pour water on the thirsty land and rivers on the dry ground. I will pour out My Spirit on your children, and will bring good to your children's children."

Lesson 7:

MARRIAGE

SCRIPTURE
MEMORIZATION

Ephesians 5:2, NIV

"Wives, submit to your own husbands as to the Lord."

the study

SUBMISSION, this word means:

_____

_____

_____

_____

_____

_____

_____

Many women cringe when they hear the word "submission." Why do you think that is?

_____

_____

_____

_____

"Submission is not about authority and it is not obedience; it is all about relationships of love and respect."
—Quote from *The Shack*

The heart of submission is truly filled with love and respect.

Ephesians 5:21, The Message
"Out of respect for Christ, be courteously reverent to one another."

WRITE how this would address the relationship with your husband.

_____

_____

_____

_____

_____

REFER to page 60 in *Excellence*.

List the three points of submission in a marriage.
I. _____
2. _____
3. _____

These three points of submission begin to be developed at what point in the couple's relationship?

_____

Write out the experience of your courtship with your spouse. Point out significant experiences that lead you to submission in the relationship.

_____

_____

_____

_____

REFER to page 61 in *Excellence*.

Married life is a workout! Putting effort forward early builds a strong foundation for the marriage. It makes for a _____. Being a good leader takes time to develop. Be patient with your husband. We all make mistakes and the words of "_____" just don't belong in our vocabulary.

Peter 3:1, NKJV

"Wives, likewise, be submissive to your own husbands, that even if some do not obey the word, they, without a word, may be won by the conduct of their wives."

WRITE a personal story when your conduct reflected the words of this scripture.

_____

_____

_____

_____

Even when it isn't easy, never give up. Stay the course of excellence in your marriage relationship. It is never too late to develop these attributes in your marriage.

promise

Ephesians 5:31, NKJV

"For this reason a man shall leave his father and mother and be joined to his wife, and the two shall become one flesh."

blessing

2 Thessalonians 3:5, NIV

"May the Lord direct your hearts into God's love and Christ's perseverance."

Lesson 8:

COMMUNITY

SCRIPTURE
MEMORIZATION

Ruth 1:16, CEV

"I will live where you live."(Ruth's statement of commitment to community.)

Mark 12:33, NIV
"Love your neighbor."

the study

The commitment to community is the third step in building the foundation that leads to a life of excellence.

Utilizing your career and community service can be your outreach or mission field that will give you a platform to put your foundation and faith into action. Having a job also affords you room to challenge yourself, to exercise your God-given talents, and to share God's love.

REFER to pages 66-68 in *Excellence*.

Having a career, serving in your church, and being active in your community can bring so much more _____ to your life when you are first mindful of your priority to _____.

Living these parts of your life outside of the home can serve to remind you of a _____.

Each job or act of service is God's way of preparing you for _____ responsibilities. _____ will be everlasting if all pursuits are done with _____. Your commitment will also allow others to experience _____ when you allow God to use you.

WRITE the quote from *Beyond Jabez* by Bruce Wilkinson.

_____

_____

_____

_____

From the book on page 68, CHOOSE three questions to answer, describing an account when you demonstrated these attributes in community. (We will not be sharing these thoughts.)

_____

_____

_____

_____

Remember the words of Dr. Bill Anderson, "God did not call us to have lots of friends, but to be a friend."

Your assignment for this year:

Become a mentor and be mentored.

This year, commit to mentor another woman, perhaps someone younger than yourself.

Then commit to being mentored by another woman who is older than yourself.

Come ready to share your plan of mentorship.

Keep a journal: keep writings of the experience of mentoring and being mentored.

promise

1 Corinthians 13:4-8, NKJV

"Love suffers long and is kind; love does not envy; love does not parade itself, is not puffed up; does not behave rudely, does not seek its own, is not provoked, thinks no evil; does not rejoice in iniquity, but rejoices in the truth; bears all things, believes all things, hopes all things, endures all things. Love never fails."

blessing

Deuteronomy 28:3-6, NKJV

"Blessed shall you be in the city, and blessed shall you be in the country.

"Blessed shall be the fruit of your body, the produce of your ground and the increase of your herds, the increase of your cattle and the offspring of your flocks.

"Blessed shall be your basket and your kneading bowl.

"Blessed shall you be when you come in, and blessed shall you be when you go out."

Lesson 9:

GOAL SETTING— *foundation* AND SPIRITUAL HEALTH

SCRIPTURE
MEMORIZATION

Habakkuk 2:2, NKJV

"Take the vision, write it down, make it plain so that you can run with it."

Goal

Execute   Assessment

Objectives

the study

Living with intentionality and purpose will put you on the path to excellence. The purpose of the following worksheet is to provide direction in your spiritual life. Pinpoint some areas of vision in your life regarding your faith, family, and community (career or volunteer endeavors). WRITE them down and create a precise strategy to help you turn those lifelong goals into reality.

REFER to pages 146-149 in *Excellence with Simple Elegance,* and refresh your mind about goal setting, process of assessment, determining objectives, and the path of how to execute the goal.

47

Short Term Goals (1-5 years)

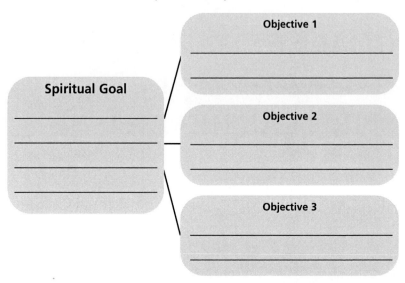

Spiritual Goal

Objective 1

Objective 2

Objective 3

Long Term Goals (5-10 years)

Spiritual Goal

Objective 1

Objective 2

Objective 3

promise

2 Peter 1:3, NLT

"By his divine power, God has given us everything we need for living a godly life. We have received all of this by coming to know him, the one who called us to himself by means of his marvelous glory and excellence."

blessing

Romans 1:7b, NLT

"May God our Father and the Lord Jesus Christ give you grace and peace."

Lesson 10:

THE HEART OF
excellence

SCRIPTURE
MEMORIZATION
Proverbs 14:30, NKJV
"A sound heart is life to the body."

the study

REFER to page 69 in *Excellence.*

Having a servant's heart is a key to a life of excellence. When LIFE BECOMES UNFAIR, you must draw from the elements of the heart. A heart that draws its strength from _____, a heart that pumps from _____, and a heart that flows with _____ will be the heart that receives _____ excellence.

WRITE your story about when life has seemed to treat you unfairly.

_____

_____

_____

_____

SHARE a scripture that gave you strength during this difficult time.

_____

_____

_____

Was your heart healed? WRITE about the healing process.

_____

_____

_____

promise

Proverbs 15:15, NLV

"All the days of the suffering are hard, but a glad heart has a special supper all the time."

blessing

Psalm 20:4, NIV

"May He give you the desire of your heart and make all your plans succeed."

Lesson 11:

BECOMING A WOMAN
OF *prayer*

SCRIPTURE
MEMORIZATION

Jeremiah 29:12,
The Message

*"When you call on me,
when you come and pray
to me, I'll listen."*

the study

Adjusting my prayer time to quiet moments alone was so out of my comfort zone. Looking back, I see how my life was similar to the struggle of Martha.

Are you a Martha or Mary? READ their story in *Luke 10*.

WRITE how you are either like Martha or Mary. SHARE your attributes as it concerns your worship, quiet time, and prayer life.

_____

_____

_____

_____

_____

A simple format for prayer is A.C.T.S.

A IS FOR ADORATION: A TIME OF PRAISING GOD FOR WHO HE IS, HIS ATTRIBUTES, HIS NAME, AND HIS CHARACTER.

C IS FOR CONFESSION: A TIME TO CONFESS YOUR SINS AND TO ASK FORGIVENESS.

T IS FOR THANKSGIVING: A TIME TO BLESS THE LORD, THANKING HIM FOR ALL HE HAS DONE FOR YOU.

S IS FOR SUPPLICATION: A TIME TO SUBMIT YOUR PRAYER LIST.

USE this format this week during your daily prayer time.

FIND a Bible verse that encourages each portion of your prayer.

ADORATION _____

CONFESSION _____

THANKSGIVING _____

SUPPLICATION _____

ROUTINE AND HABIT ARE THE KEYS TO EXCELLENCE IN PRAYER LIFE.

1 Thessalonians 5:17, NKJV
"...Pray without ceasing."

Make it a habit to take God with you everywhere you go; don't leave Him out of anything. Prayer is not dictated by place and time. Its place is everywhere; its time is any time.

WRITE about different places and times you have spent time in prayer.

_____

_____

_____

_____

_____

_____

_____

_____

PRAYER JOURNAL

BUY a notebook you exclusively designate for prayers.

WRITE your needs and the prayer requests of others in the journal. Also LIST how God answers each petition.

_____

_____

_____

_____

Matthew 6:5-13, NKJV The Model Prayer

"And when you pray, you shall not be like the hypocrites. For they love to pray standing in the synagogues and on the corners of the streets, that

they may be seen by men. Assuredly, I say to you, they have their reward.

But you, when you pray, go into your room, and when you have shut your door, pray to your Father who is in the secret place; and your Father who sees in secret will reward you openly. And when you pray, do not use vain repetitions as the heathen do. For they think that they will be heard for their many words.

"Therefore do not be like them. For your Father knows the things you have need of before you ask Him. In this manner, therefore, pray:

'Our Father in heaven,
Hallowed be Your name.
Your kingdom come.
Your will be done
On earth as it is in heaven.
Give us this day our daily bread.
And forgive us our debts,
As we forgive our debtors.
And do not lead us into temptation,
But deliver us from the evil one.
For Yours is the kingdom and the power and the glory forever. Amen.'"

promise

Matthew 7:7, NKJV

"Ask, and it will be given to you; seek, and you will find; knock, and it will be opened to you."

blessing

Psalm 20:1-2,5, Adapted from the NIV

"May the LORD answer you when you are in distress; may the name of the God of Jacob protect you. May he send you help and grant you support. May the LORD grant all your requests."

Lesson 12:

SIMPLE *grace*

SCRIPTURE
MEMORIZATION

Ephesians 2:8, NKJV

*"For by grace you have
been saved through faith
and not of yourselves; it
is the gift of God."*

the study

DEFINE the word grace.

_____

_____

_____

_____

_____

_____

_____

There are four main roles of the grace
of God. See page 76 of *Excellence*.

1. _____

_____

_____

_____

2. _____

_____

_____

_____

3. _____

_____

4. _____

_____

WRITE a story in your life in which you have experienced God's grace.

_____

_____

_____

_____

_____

_____

_____

_____

How many times have you heard friends and family say they don't want to be a part of faith, church, or religion because of the "dos" and "don'ts"? SHARE your experiences around this issue.

_____

_____

_____

_____

_____

Our faith walk is definitely dictated by our willingness to be obedient to God. And it is not troublesome because... (based on 1 John 5:3)

_____

_____

_____

_____

The beauty of obedience is that experiencing His grace and His love in return makes whatever sacrifice we made appear small in comparison to His grace and to the power of God in your life. These are the vehicles that drive you to the place of excellence.

promise

Psalm 145:8, CEV

"You are merciful, LORD! You are kind and patient and always loving."

blessing

2 Corinthians 13:11,14, NIV

"And the God of love and peace will be with you....

"May the grace of the Lord Jesus Christ, and the love of God, and the fellowship of the Holy Spirit be with you all."

Lesson 13:

SIMPLY *forgive*

Scripture
Memorization

Mark 11:25, NLT

"But when you are praying, first forgive anyone you are holding a grudge against, so that your Father in heaven will forgive your sins, too."

the study

Forgiveness is not a feeling, but a decision. A life of excellence comes with a forgiving heart. Somehow we have developed the idea that when we forgive, we are doing something wonderful for the person we are forgiving. In reality, forgiveness for others is what's best for ourselves.

REFER to page 79 in *Excellence* to fill in the blanks on forgiveness.

We need to forgive but also we need forgiveness. So many people make mistakes that they regret for the rest of their lives. Without a doubt, that's why God created forgiveness. He made a way for us to start anew— a way called _____

_____

_____

_____

_____.

Job 33:26, NKJV

"For He restores to man His righteousness."

It is never too late to set your path straight. There's no better time to get your _____ and _____ in order. That place is where freedom lives.

WRITE about a time when it was hard for you to forgive.

_____

_____

_____

_____

_____

_____

Just as forgiveness sets you free, a lack of forgiveness creates resentment that will eat away at the contentment in your life. The feelings generated from that absence of forgiveness will occupy our minds, interfere with our ability to build our foundation, and reestablish our commitment to God daily.

WRITE about a time when it was easy for you to forgive.

_____

_____

_____

_____

FIND four scripture verses where we are instructed to forgive.

WRITE out *Matthew 18:22*.

_____

_____

_____

_____

_____

WRITE about a time you needed forgiveness and you received it. Express the freedom you experienced. (We will not be sharing this story.)

_____

_____

_____

_____

WRITE about a time that you needed forgiveness and you were not forgiven by the one you offended. (We will not be sharing this story.)

_____

_____

_____

_____

_____

WRITE about an offense for which you have not forgiven yourself.

_____

_____

_____

_____

The promise of forgiveness: FIND four scripture verses that assure us God forgives.

_____

_____

_____

_____

Begin resetting your _____ on
_____ principles today.

Choosing a life of faith and living it in excellence always comes with sacrifice.

NAME sacrifices you have made to live a righteous life.

_____

_____

_____

_____

promise

Luke 6:35-38, NLV

"But love those who hate you. Do good to them. Let them use your things and do not expect something back. Your reward will be much. You will be the children of the Most High. He is kind to those who are not thankful and to those who are full of sin. You must have loving-kindness just as your Father has loving-kindness. Do not say what is wrong in other people's lives. Then other people will not say what is wrong in your life. Do not say someone is guilty. Then other people will not say you are guilty. Forgive other people and other people will forgive you. Give, and it will be given to you. You will have more than enough. It can be pushed down and shaken together and it will still run over as it is given to you. The way you give to others is the way you will receive in return."

blessing

Psalm 121:5-8, NIV

"The LORD watches over you—
the LORD is your shade at your right hand;
the sun will not harm you by day,
nor the moon by night.

The LORD will keep you from all harm—
he will watch over your life;
the LORD will watch over your coming and going
both now and forevermore."

Lesson 14:

GOAL SETTING—ISSUES OF THE *heart* AND EMOTIONAL HEALTH

SCRIPTURE
MEMORIZATION

Psalm 20:4, NKJV

"May He grant
you according to your
heart's desire,

and fulfill all
your purpose."

the study

A goal is a measurable, attainable aspiration in a specific period of your life. The purpose of the following worksheet is to provide direction concerning your prayer life, worship, and Bible reading. Making positive steps toward the healing of parts of our lives can hurt. Step toward being a woman of excellence by praying without ceasing, forgiving daily, and extending grace by the power of knowing your heavenly Father will propel you toward a life of emotional health.

SHORT TERM GOALS (1-5 YEARS)

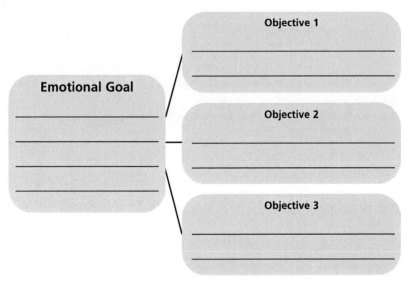

Objective 1

Emotional Goal

Objective 2

Objective 3

LONG TERM GOALS (5-10 YEARS)

Objective 1

Emotional Goal

Objective 2

Objective 3

promise

Psalm 112:3, NLV

"Riches and well-being are in his house. And his right-standing with God will last forever."

blessing

1 Corinthians 1:3, NLT

"May God our Father and the Lord Jesus Christ give you grace and peace."

THE INGREDIENTS OF
excellence

SCRIPTURE
MEMORIZATION

Deuteronomy 6:18,
NLT

*"Do what is right and
good in the Lord's sight,
so all will go well
with you."*

the study

GOD HAS CALLED US TO EXCELLENCE. ONE MIGHT FIND THE TASK OF CREATING AND MAINTAINING A LIFE OF EXCELLENCE TO BE A DAUNTING ONE, AND IT CAN BE IF WE DO NOT UNDERSTAND MOST IMPORTANTLY THAT EXCELLENCE IS A JOURNEY.

It takes time, energy, and willingness in this journey to achieve excellence and to acquire the ingredients that comprise it. Once you have established that you are on a journey, it is important to realize what it will take to get there.

In this journey you will need three primary ingredients. See page 84 of *Excellence*.

_____, _____,

and _____.

WRITE why you believe these three primary ingredients are necessary in the pursuit of excellence in your life.

_____

_____

_____

_____

WRITE a prayer asking God to guide and to give you strength in this journey to excellence.

_____

_____

_____

_____

promise

Isaiah 43:2, NLV

"When you pass through the waters, I will be with you. When you pass through the rivers, they will not flow over you. When you walk through the fire, you will not be burned. The fire will not destroy you."

blessing

Psalm 106:3, NIV

"Blessed are those who act justly, who always do what is right."

Lesson 16:

COURAGE

SCRIPTURE
MEMORIZATION

Colossians 3:23,
NKJV

"Whatever you do, do it heartily as to the Lord and not to men."

the study

Reference the quote from the *New Spirit-Filled Bible;* what does this mean to you?

"Know that God grants seasons of favor for His people in order to extend His kingdom."

_____

_____

_____

_____

_____

_____

_____

_____

_____

READ the story of Queen Esther. You will find her story in the book of Esther in The Old Testament.

See page 85 in *Excellence*.

Esther means _____.
Why do you think the meaning of her name is significant?

_____

_____

_____

_____

_____

Scripture says she was ordained to fulfill God's purpose.
"_____

_____," *Esther 4:14.*

How does this familiar and popular statement have signifi-
cance for you today?

_____

_____

_____

Esther possessed great beauty and loveliness. But what did Esther
have more than all of the other young ladies in her village?

_____

_____

_____

_____

You must believe that God has a wonderful purpose for your life, one that is significant and important. God has also blessed you just like Queen Esther with an innate ability/gift. WRITE what you believe your abilities and gifts are.

_____

_____

_____

_____

_____

Esther possessed all the right ingredients to fulfill God's purpose. By God's sovereignty and Esther's courage, the door was opened. EXPLAIN how God has opened doors for you, how you had courage, and were obedient in using your gifts.

_____

_____

_____

_____

_____

Mordecai (cousin to Esther and the one who raised her) called Esther to her mission. The words that Mordecai spoke into her life brought her to the realization of her significant life-mission.

Do you have someone in your life that challenges you to seek out your destiny? Do you have someone who is motivating you to discover your significant life-mission? SHARE.

_____

_____

_____

_____

_____

If you do know your calling, what steps have you taken to fulfill God's call?

_____

_____

_____

_____

_____

"If I perish, I perish," were the words spoken by Esther. A risk of death was the sacrifice she would have to face in obedience to the call on her life to save the Jewish nation.

What sacrifice have you made in your life in obedience to God's call on your life?

_____

_____

_____

_____

_____

Esther acted intelligently and with courage. Write how Esther demonstrates these characteristics.

_____

_____

_____

_____

_____

Just as God did for Esther, God will reward you with His favor. Esther's courage resulted in the deliverance of God's people. Your courage will make the difference in your world.

Write a testament to God's favor in your life that was a direct result of your courage.

_____

_____

_____

_____

_____

Commit to walk your journey to excellence with purpose and courage.

promise

Joshua 1:9, NKJV

"Be strong and of good courage; do not be afraid, nor be dismayed, for the LORD your God is with you wherever you go."

blessing

Psalm 119, The Message

"You're blessed when you stay on course, walking steadily on the road revealed by God.

You're blessed when you follow his directions,
doing your best to find him.
That's right—you don't go off on your own;
you walk straight along the road he set.
You, God, prescribed the right way to live;
now you expect us to live it.
Oh, that my steps might be steady,
keeping to the course you set;
Then I'd never have any regrets
in comparing my life with your counsel.
I thank you for speaking straight from your heart;
I learn the pattern of your righteous ways.
I'm going to do what you tell me to do;
don't ever walk off and leave me."

Lesson 17:

PASSION

SCRIPTURE
MEMORIZATION

Ephesians 6:7, NLT

*"Work with enthusiasm,
as though you were
working for the Lord
rather than for people."*

the study

REFER to pages 90-91 in *Excellence*.

Passion is _____
_____
_____
_____.

Passion is an object of _____
_____ or
_____ interest.

It is often that our _____
interest might change with _____
_____ seasons
of our life. Learn to be _____
and _____ new passions.

Love what you do and do what
you love.

God has called all believers to serve others. It is imperative to develop a "_____."

When you realize that life is not about you but others, life begins to _____.

WRITE about what you love to do that is in the realm of serving others.

_____

_____

_____

Passion allows endeavors of life to be enjoyable, fun, and creative.

Passion takes away the mundane repetitive motion of just doing the work.

WRITE about a repetitive motion that has become mundane.

_____

_____

Now with *Ephesians 6:7* in mind, how can you do this work with enthusiasm?

_____

_____

_____

REMIND yourself: If you can harness that strong feeling—passion—toward the endeavors of your life, you will find JOY, CONTENTMENT, AND FULFILLMENT.

Many chores are required of us that we don't have passion for the work. Think about why you are doing it and who you are doing it for. WRITE your thoughts.

_____

_____

_____

It is in the "why" that we are passionate.

Career change! If you have lost the zeal for a job, USE the goal-setting session to write a plan to change your career; writing specifically what you need to do to make the move to a new career.

Make sure your passion starts strong and remains strong to ensure you're not only a great "starter" but also a great "finisher" at achieving excellence. Without passion, commitment is weak.

It is a must to finish STRONG. The work has your name on it and we are a direct representation of God in this world. Your actions speak louder about your faith than your words.

PASSIONATE LIVES ARE GREAT LIVES! MAKE YOUR LIFE GREAT!

promise

Psalm 37:4, NKJV

"Delight yourself also in the LORD, And He shall give you the desires of your heart."

blessing

Psalm 115:15, NLT

"May you be blessed by the LORD, Who made heaven and earth."

Lesson 18:

DISCIPLINE

SCRIPTURE
MEMORIZATION

Galatians 6:9, KJV

"And let us not be weary in well doing: for in due season we shall reap, if we faint not."

the study

REFER to page 90 in *Excellence.*

Discipline means _____
_____
_____
_____
_____
_____
_____
_____
_____
_____.

Even after you have set a format for your life that aligns with God's Word and will, it is not always an easy path to stay on. Life provides hundreds of opportunities that challenge us to look at our decisions, to evaluate and adjust. In short, A LIFE OF EXCELLENCE TAKES DISCIPLINE.

Having clear dreams and goals within the format of your life can give you great momentum and direction. Choosing to sidestep boundaries by making a wrong choice because it appears easy and gratifying can be short-lived and painful. The decisions we make for ourselves will affect us through-out our entire lives. IF OUR GOAL REALLY IS EXCELLENCE, WE NEED TO BE PREPARED TO STAY THE COURSE.

From *Proverbs 31* we learn what a virtuous and disciplined lifestyle should look like for us as women.

This passage is from the NIV translation. LOOK UP THE ACTION WORDS AND FILL IN THE BLANKS; these describe disci-pline and give you a good picture of discipline and hard work.

This passage says of the virtuous woman:
"Her worth is far above rubies. She _____
for her husband and not evil. She willingly _____
with her hands and _____ food for her household.
She _____ a field and _____ it.
Then from her profits she _____ a vineyard.

"She _____ herself and _____ her
arms. Her lamp _____ by night. She
_____ her hands to the spinning wheel and
her hand _____ the spindle. She _____
her hand to the poor and _____ her hands to the
needy. Her household _____ with scarlet and
she even _____ tapestry for herself. Her clothing _____ linen and purple. She _____

linen garments, _____ them, and _____ sashes for the merchants. Strength and honor are her clothing. She _____ *her mouth with wisdom*, so her tongue is the law of kindness. She _____ over the ways of her household, and _____ the bread of idleness."

I believe we need to make a life-altering decision to be this disciplined. From the virtuous woman we see the necessity of developing a pattern of behavior of discipline that exhibits *hard work*.

The author of Proverbs plainly spells it out: *this* is what a hard worker looks like. The excellent woman realizes that her boss is her heavenly Father and she does everything as unto Him.

Our reward for being disciplined and hard working: Scripture promises heavenly rewards. WRITE two verses that speak to our rewards.

_____

_____

_____

_____

USE the goal-setting session to establish DISCIPLINE in your life where it is lacking.

Our lives will be enriched when we exercise the qualities of courage, passion, and DISCIPLINE. If we are patient and diligent with what God has entrusted to us, nurturing it the best we know how, we will grow into women of excellence.

promise

Matthew 11:28, The Living Bible

"Come to me and I will give you rest—all of you who work so hard."

blessing

Jude 1:24, 25, NKJV

"Now to Him who is able to keep you from stumbling, and to present you faultless before the presence of His glory with exceeding joy, to God our Savior, Who alone is wise, be glory and majesty, dominion and power, both now and forever. Amen."

Lesson 19:

GOAL SETTING— INGREDIENTS OF *excellence* AND MENTAL HEALTH

SCRIPTURE
MEMORIZATION

2 Timothy 1:7, NIV

"God did not give us a spirit of timidity, but a spirit of power, of love, and of self-discipline."

the study

These specific ingredients (courage, passion, and discipline) we must possess to become the best version of ourselves. Many people never make positive steps to improvement because they think it's too hard or they simply do not know how to begin. To be honest with you, it is hard to become proficient where we lack proficiency. But it is attainable if you know these goals are worth the sacrifice. Remember that God has given you the ability to accomplish your goals; you just have to believe that you can learn and do it. Get passionate about them! Effective effort really counts!

Short Term Goals (1-5 years)

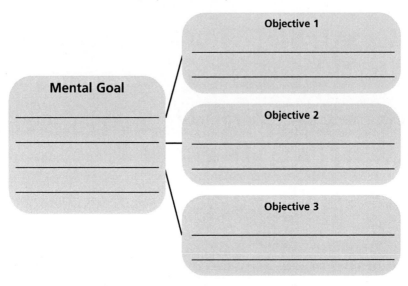

Mental Goal
_____
_____
_____
_____

Objective 1
_____
_____

Objective 2
_____
_____

Objective 3
_____
_____

Long Term Goals (5-10 years)

Mental Goal
_____
_____
_____
_____

Objective 1
_____
_____

Objective 2
_____
_____

Objective 3
_____
_____

promise

Psalms 84:11, NLT

"For the Lord God is our sun and our shield.
He gives us grace and glory.
The Lord will withhold no good thing
from those who do what is right."

blessing

Galatians 1:3, CEV

"I pray that God the Father and our Lord Jesus Christ will be kind to you and will bless you with peace!"

Lesson 20:

SEASONS OF *life*

SCRIPTURE MEMORIZATION

Psalm 37:4, NKJV

"Delight yourself also in the Lord, and he shall give you the desires of your heart."

1 Chronicles 4:10, NIV

"Jabez cried out to the God of Israel, 'Oh, that you would bless me and enlarge my territory! Let your hand be with me, and keep me from harm so that I will be free from pain.' And God granted his request."

the study

UNDERSTAND THE SEASON.

Like the seasons of nature—winter, spring, summer, and fall—so are the seasons of life.

Seasons are specific periods of time, and they vary in length. The opportunities of one season are not always available in another. And each season will prepare you for the next.

READ *Ecclesiastes 3:1-8*

Seasons are birthed out of three specific reasons. WRITE the three reasons from page 103 in *Excellence*.

1.

2.

3.

EXCELLENCE *with* SIMPLE ELEGANCE

When we recognize the seasons we are in and exercise wisdom in them, we can experience all that God desires for us in that season.

IDENTIFY the season you are in.

_____

_____

_____

_____

_____

EXPLAIN what you believe God desires for you in this season.

_____

_____

_____

_____

WRITE the routine that you have in place that makes this season fulfilling.

_____

_____

_____

_____

How have you made your life simple so you can grasp all that God has for you in this season? SHARE.

_____

_____

_____

_____

_____

PREPARE FOR THE SEASON

It is our human nature to hang on to some seasons, even when God is ready to move us to another one. New seasons can bring many emotions.

WRITE the emotions you have felt in this new season of your life and how you did or did not prepare for this season.

_____

_____

_____

_____

_____

_____

_____

_____

_____

SHARE scripture that has had an impact on your life during the season you are experiencing right now.

_____

_____

_____

_____

_____

_____

PURPOSE FOR THE SEASONS

There is purpose in every season. SHARE the purpose for this season you are now experiencing.

_____

_____

_____

_____

As women, we often have an innate need to be able to do and be many things. But recognize that there is an order to maintain and a specific season in your life to do it.

Each season offers you great knowledge, wisdom, and opportunity to be educated for what lies ahead in your life. Don't miss any season in your life, as that will also be an opportunity missed.

Many opportunities come knocking on your life's door.

IDENTIFY the three questions from page 113 in *Excellence* that assist you in making a decision to embark on an opportunity.

1.

2.

3.

TALK ABOUT A TIME in your life when you totally missed a wonderful opportunity.

_____

_____

_____

_____

_____

WRITE a Plan of Action: Comprised of steps that you will take to determine whether a proposed opportunity is God's will for your life and for this season of your life.

_____

_____

_____

_____

_____

In this present season, are you in the center of God's will and call on your life? If the answer is no, WRITE a letter to yourself convincing yourself to get back on track with the path God has for you.

_____

_____

_____

_____

PRAY the Prayer of Jabez daily. God will expand your territory if that is your heart's desire.

promise

Psalm 84:10-11, NLT

"A single day in your courts is better than a thousand anywhere else!

"I would rather be a gatekeeper in the house of my God than live the good life in the homes of the wicked.

"For the Lord God is our sun and our shield. He gives us grace and glory. The Lord will withhold no good thing from those who do what is right."

blessing

2 Peter 1:2, The Message

"Grace and peace to you many times over as you deepen in your experience with God."

Lesson 21:

SIMPLE *elegance*

SCRIPTURE
MEMORIZATION

1 Corinthians 6:19,
NLT

*"Don't you realize that
your body is the temple of
the Holy Spirit, who lives
in you and was given to
you by God?"*

Psalm 139:14, NKJV

*"I will praise You, for I
am fearfully and wonder-
fully made; marvelous are
Your works, and that my
soul knows very well."*

the study

For most women, the way you look can greatly affect how you feel. When a woman doesn't look successful, put together, confident, and beautiful, she most likely won't feel that way either. The simple plan for excellence will allow you to pursue life's challenges with confidence.

God's goodness should overflow and shine outwardly from you. It is so important that we bring the elegance, tenderness, and simplicity of womanhood to our world.

A mirror is a household object that gives an honest reflection. Is the mirror in your home revealing an image you are happy with? Is it a true representation of who you really are or want to be? SHARE YOUR ANSWER.

_____

_____

_____

The best way to begin improving your reflection is to make a routine for yourself that includes attention to each and every part of you. We all have the ability to look our "best self." You must believe that God has created beauty in you. So now is the opportunity you absolutely need to take the steps to let all of it shine.

A SIMPLE PLAN OF ACTION TO ELEGANCE
TAKE CARE OF YOUR BODY.

READ Song of Solomon, chapters four and five. This is a groom describing every part of his bride's body. He adores her. All women want be seen like this in the eyes of their lover. So let's get to work! If you are in great shape now with little effort, know that maintenance of what you possess needs attention daily. So begin today taking care of the physical outside and inside of your body.

Create a routine of exercise. Schedule 30 minutes of exercise four days each week and reserve one day for recreational activity.

Plan menus of healthy foods. Remove the junk food and processed food from your home and replace with low-sugar, low-fat, and unprocessed foods. Keep in mind foods that have brilliant color will provide the best nutrition for your body. Increase and put emphasis on your fruit and vegetable intake over your meat intake. Get rid of the sodas and juices—Drink WATER. Remove the white breads and pasta; replace with whole wheat. This will be a good start to nutritional health. Always consult with a dietitian for special dietary needs.

READ Esther 2:1-18.

Start a skin care routine. When your skin looks great, you are always putting your best face forward. Get into a routine of cleansing, toning, and moisturizing twice a day, morning and night. Look for dermatologist-recommended products. Don't neglect the rest of your body skin care. Include perfumes, body lotions, toothpaste/whitener, mouthwash, and, my favorite, bubble bath.

Schedule a spa day. This day could include an at-home treatment or professional treatment. Your spa day needs to include a manicure, pedicure, hair treatment/style, and makeup application. Note: For group study, this spa day could be part of a meeting.

Focus on wardrobe, apparel and accessories. Go through your closet and get rid of items that you have not worn in 12 months (with exception of formal and holiday wear) and the apparel that does not fit. Get in a habit of purchasing a personal wardrobe that contains timeless pieces.

Your pursuit of excellence in physical health will begin when you start by asking yourself: Who are you physically? Who do you want to realistically become? SHARE YOUR ANSWERS.

_____

_____

_____

When we are our best physical self, we free up our minds and hearts to be more dedicated to God. We can physically do what God has called us to do because we have done our part to be physically healthy.

What matters to you also matters to God because He cares for you.

promise

1 Peter 5:7, NKJV

"Casting all your care upon Him, for He cares for you."

blessing

Philemon 1:25, NKJV

"The grace of our Lord Jesus Christ be with your spirit. Amen."

Lesson 22:

THE GUEST-READY *home*

SCRIPTURE
MEMORIZATION

Proverbs 31:28, NKJV

"Her children rise up and call her blessed; Her husband also."

the study

The scene was set: food, live entertainment, candles, flowers, white linens, and 250 guests meandering in and around our home. In the midst of the party I fielded the question that prompted the writing of my book, *Excellence with Simple Elegance.* "How do you do it?" The answer is *keep life simple.*

Simple and *routine* are the keys words to maintaining your home. Keeping one's home is a huge task but a necessary one. A routine that is well-rehearsed is crucial to keeping the stress level low each day and maintaining a clean, tidy home. Simplicity (not extravagance) is the key to unlocking joy into your physical living space.

Excellence needs to be applied to the way you keep your home and the things you own. Good stewardship is an important part of being a woman of faith. A good steward is one who deals wisely with what God has entrusted to them and takes good care to protect it. The idea of stewardship should be applied to everything we have—all of our possessions.

A FEW WAYS TO KEEP LIFE SIMPLE

Clear the clutter. We possess far too much stuff. Dispose of the piles of unnecessary items (papers, broken and worn out items, and all things you never use) that clutter your living space, closets/cabinets, garage, and basement. *Keep only what you really need.* The rule is if you haven't used it in a year; you never will use it! Organize a garage sale with the study group. Give funds raised to a ministry within the church or community.

Organize your storage areas including the closets, cabinets, and basements. If you don't know where to start, find someone who has a knack for organization and have them assist you. Keep those areas neat, tidy, and organized by eliminating items that are unnecessary on a daily basis.

Housekeeping: Schedule each area to be cleaned on a specific day during spring and fall. Clean thoroughly. This is intense cleaning done only once or twice a year.

Maintenance: Outside maintenance of your yard and the exterior of the home should be scheduled during months that weather permits. Keep the adornments of your lawn and gardens simple so you can maintain excellence easily. Find cleaning products that easily bring a sparkle to your siding and windows.

Indoor maintenance: This becomes easier when you have embraced the tradition of "spring housekeeping" which is the intense deep cleaning. Create a routine of daily maintenance.

BRING your calendar to the group to share your proposed routine for accomplishing the guest-ready home. COME ready to share but also to be open to new ideas. We want a routine that is quick and easy so we can spend more time with our family, with friends, in service to others, in ministry, and having fun experiencing the abundant life that God has for us.

If you share my belief that all good things come from God, then daily tasks of maintenance become more than that; they take the form of stewardship for the things He has given us. Even in the caretaking of our homes and things God has blessed us with, He can be glorified.

promise
James 1:17, CEV

"Every good and perfect gift comes from the Father who created all the lights in heavens. He is always the same...."

blessing

3 John 1:2, NKJV

"Beloved, I pray that you may prosper in all things and be in health, just as your soul prospers."

Lesson 23:

TIME *management*

SCRIPTURE MEMORIZATION

Ecclesiastes 3:1, NLV

"There is a special time for everything. There is a time for everything that happens under heaven."

the study

Time is the most precious commodity we possess. Use it wisely!

A morally excellent woman is disciplined, organized, and orderly. A woman of excellence has a prescribed conduct or pattern of behavior that is productive and above reproach. Time management is the key to achieving a life of excellence, and being disciplined is the key to time management.

Let's get started and finish well. In this session, set hourly, daily, weekly, and monthly goals for yourself. Prioritize each task and each appointment.

Categories to address in your monthly calendar: (use any monthly planner)

The Menu

Appointment/Events

Exercise/Recreation

Quiet Time

Spa/Salon

Decorating Home

Date Night with Spouse

Family Time and Family Vacations

INFORM YOUR FAMILY OF THE UPCOMING SCHEDULE. SUNDAY NIGHT, PROVIDE THE WEEKLY AGENDA FOR EACH FAMILY MEMBER MAKING SURE EVERYONE'S HOURLY RESPONSIBILITY IS ON THE WORKSHEET.

Family Week Schedule

Member	Time	Monday	Tuesday	Wednesday	Thursday	Friday	Saturday	Sunday
Dad	6:00 AM							
	9:00 AM							
	12:00 PM							
	3:00 PM							
	6:00 PM							
	9:00 PM							
Mom	6:00 AM							
	9:00 AM							
	12:00 PM							
	3:00 PM							
	6:00 PM							
	9:00 PM							
Son	6:00 AM							
	9:00 AM							
	12:00 PM							
	3:00 PM							
	6:00 PM							
	9:00 PM							
Daughter	6:00 AM							
	9:00 AM							
	12:00 PM							
	3:00 PM							
	6:00 PM							
	9:00 PM							

promise

Psalm 37:5, NKJV

"Commit your way to the LORD, trust also in Him, and He shall bring it to pass."

blessing

Matthew 5:3-10, NKJV

"Blessed are the poor in spirit,
For theirs is the kingdom of heaven.
"Blessed are those who mourn,
For they shall be comforted.
"Blessed are the meek,
For they shall inherit the earth.
"Blessed are those who hunger and thirst for righteousness,
For they shall be filled.
"Blessed are the merciful,
For they shall obtain mercy.
"Blessed are the pure in heart,
For they shall see God.
"Blessed are the peacemakers,
For they shall be called sons of God.
"Blessed are those who are persecuted for righteousness' sake,
For theirs is the kingdom of heaven."

Lesson 24:

GOAL *setting* SIMPLE ELEGANCE / GUEST-READY HOME / TIME MANAGEMENT AND PHYSICAL HEALTH

SCRIPTURE MEMORIZATION

Luke 6:23, NIV

"Rejoice in that day and leap for joy, because great is your reward in heaven."

the study

Commitment to excellence means "no compromise." It means that you deliberately apply action to what you believe. It is a pledge to do what you set out to do, no matter the sacrifice it requires. It's living with integrity and consistency. Being intentional in all things. It is being connected to something bigger than you. It is staying strong in your conviction when it's no longer convenient or easy. Commitment is easy to talk about, but challenging to put into action. It takes an incredible amount of discipline to stay on course. Knowing this, get an accountable partner to hold you to your physical goals; this will lead to personal success. Be a finisher of the goals you put in place.

SHORT TERM GOALS (1-5 YEARS)

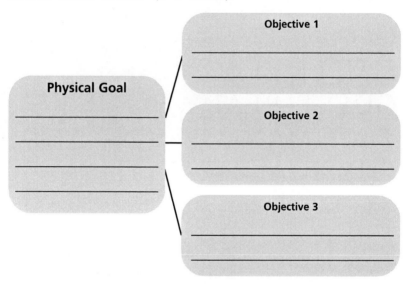

LONG TERM GOALS (5-10 YEARS)

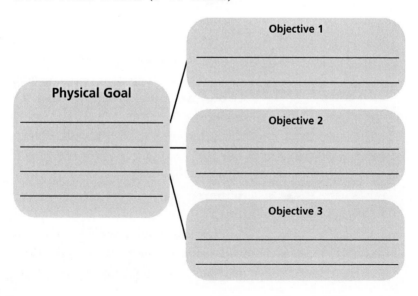

MY COMMITMENT

WRITE a paragraph about why you are committed to excellence in your life and what motivated you to make this commitment.

_____

_____

_____

_____

_____

_____

promise

1 John 5:20, NLV

"We know God's Son has come. He has given us the understanding to know Him Who is the true God. We are joined together with the true God through His Son, Jesus Christ. He is the true God and the life that lasts forever."

blessing

2 Corinthians 13:13

"May God bless you with his love."

TO CONTACT THE AUTHOR

Bonnie welcomes the opportunity to spread words of encouragement to readers across the country. For speaking engagements including women's conferences and events, contact Bonnie at bliabenow@live.com.

Core Communications
409 Wedgewood Drive
Cadillac, Michigan 49601

Phone: (231) 499-7580

Website: coreleaders.net

facebook.com/bonnieliabenow

Blog site: bonnieliabenow.com